Presented to: Elizabeth

From: Alexandra

HAPPY
VALENTINE'S
DAY
1999

*B*e strong and brave . . . I will be
with you everywhere you go.

—Joshua 1:9

Bible Promises for Kids
Copyright 1998 by the Zondervan Corporation
ISBN: 0-310-97696-0

Excerpts taken from:

The Kids' Devotional Bible: New International Version
Copyright 1996 by the Zondervan Corporation
All rights reserved.

The Holy Bible: New International Version
Copyright 1973, 1978, 1984 by International Bible Society

Requests for information should be addressed to:

ZondervanPublishingHouse
Mail Drop B20
Grand Rapids, Michigan 49530
http://www.zondervan.com

Senior Editor: Gwen Ellis
Compiler: Candy Paull
Design: Mark Veldheer

Printed in the United States of America
98 99 00 01/DP/ 8 7 6 5 4 3 2 1

He has chosen you to
share life with his Son,
Jesus Christ our Lord.

—1 Corinthians 1:9

How great is the love
the Father has given
us so freely!

—1 John 3:1

What does God call you? He calls you his *child!* That means you're related. You belong to God. What a great God! What a wonderful Father!

*I have put my rainbow
in the clouds.*

—Genesis 9:13

God said to Noah, "I promise I will never send another flood to drown you." Then God put a rainbow in the sky as a reminder of his promise.

We who have strong
faith should help the weak
with their problems.

—Romans 15:1

God likes people who *share* the goodies! Don't just stand there. Today's a great day to do something good for somebody else!

I'll put my trust in God my Savior.

—Micah 7:7

When you feel bad, find someone who can help. Someone you can talk to. God will help you. He will be with you. And he will bring you to a safe place.

Because you belong to Christ Jesus, you are all one.

—Galatians 3:28

No one is better than anyone else. God made you just the way he wanted you to be. You are equal with everyone else. God loves all his children.

We've promised to be friends.

—1 Samuel 20:42

Friends are special gifts from God. They bring joy to your life. Thank God for your friends.

Two people are better than one.

—Ecclesiastes 4:9

It is better to do things with someone else than to be all alone. Everything in life is better when someone shares it.

*He will sing with joy
because of you.*

—Zephaniah 3:17

God loves you so much he sings. Imagine that! God sings because of you!

There will be showers of blessing.

—Ezekiel 34:26

That's a great picture, isn't it? God will rain blessings gently on your head. That's how God promises to bless you. Raise your face to God. Drink in the blessings.

"You have done well, good and faithful servant! You have been faithful with a few things; I will put you in charge of many things."

—Matthew 25:21

God gives you good things.
Talent. Money. A cheerful attitude.
He trusts you to use what he gives
you to help others.

*P*ut God's kingdom first. Do what he wants you to do. Then all those things will be given you.

—Matthew 6:33

Jesus has the power to give us food, clothes, and everything we need. God is truly great!

Mighty warrior, the LORD is with you.

—Judges 6:12

God knows you. He knows what you can and cannot do. Ask God to show you how he sees you. Then watch how God will make you great.

Then you will call out to me.
You will come and pray to me.
And I will listen to you.

—Jeremiah 29:12

Through big things or small things, God works in your life. He listens to you. And he answers your prayers.

*The Lord will cover you
with his wings.*

—Psalm 91:4

God wants to take you on his lap and hold you, comfort you, and protect you. God invites you into the loving security of his arms.

Jesus answered, "I am the way and the truth and the life. No one comes to the Father except through me.

—John 14:6

The Bible says Jesus is the way to God. This way is the best way to get through life.

I am sure that the One who began a good work in you will carry it on until it is completed.

—Philippians 1:6

God never, never gives up!
God began a good work in you.
He will *never* give up until his
work is complete.

*Spend a lot of time in prayer.
Always be watchful and thankful.*

—Colossians 4:2

Ever notice how easy it is to never be satisfied? There's a simple way you can fight the greed monster. Be thankful. You will be content.

*W*ise children make their fathers glad. But foolish children bring sorrow to their mothers.

—Proverbs 10:1

Do you bring smiles to your parents, or tears? Smiles? Good! Be wise and bring joy to your parents.

"The Scriptures you study give witness about me."

—John 5:39

The Bible leads people to Jesus.
Jesus is the one who saves. Jesus is
the one who gives everlasting life.

When I kept silent about my sin,
my body became weak.

—Psalm 32:3

When you sin, don't hide it. Tell God you are sorry. God promises to forgive you. Doing these things will help you be healthy and happy.

Pay attention to the Lord's commands that I'm giving you today.

—Deuteronomy 28:13

God wants you to be first in line for a good life. He says you can be if you:

1. Know what his commands are, and

2. Obey God's commands.

He will give perfect peace to those who . . . trust in him.

—Isaiah 26:3

God will talk to you. He'll listen to your fears. He'll comfort you. He'll help you understand. He'll take time with you.

Samuel replied: "Speak. I'm listening."

—1 Samuel 3:10

You are never too young to hear God's voice. Usually God will speak to you through the Bible or through your parents. What should you do when God speaks?

51

Do what is right. Then you will be accepted.

—Genesis 4:7

It's easier to sin when you're angry. But you can choose to do right *even when* you are angry. Choose to do right. God will help you win over sin.

*His great love is new
every morning.*

—Lamentations 3:23

God never runs out of what people need.
He has enough of everything to share.
And he always has patience to spare! So
fill yourself up with his love today.

Go home to your family.
Tell them how much the Lord
has done for you.

—Mark 5:19

You know the truth. Talk about God with your friends. And God will use your knowledge in great ways!

May the LORD *answer you when you are in trouble.*

—Psalm 20:1

God hears your prayers. And nothing is too hard for God. So when you pray, get ready for your answer to come. It may almost seem too good to be true, but God will answer.

The joy of the LORD
makes you strong.

—Nehemiah 8:10

Forget your failures. Dry your tears. The joy of the Lord makes you strong. Lift your face to the sun. Smile with God. Open your heart to joy.

*Let the heavens be
filled with joy.*

—1 Chronicles 16:31

God tells the earth to praise him. The Bible often talks about a happy creation—singing stars and peace among the animals.

So cheer each other up with the hope you have. Build each other up.

—I Thessalonians 5:11

"How would I feel if I were in the new kid's shoes in school?" If you ask yourself this question you will become a better friend. That will make everyone's day happier.

Be at peace with each other.

—Mark 9:50

Peace starts with you. If you have a problem with fighting, ask Jesus to help you. Jesus will turn your hitting hands into helpful hands. Give your hands to Jesus, and see the great things you will do!

*B*ut suppose someone does sin. Then we have one who speaks to the Father for us.

—1 John 2:1

Did you ever have a friend stick up for you? It felt great, didn't it? Jesus is like that friend. He will always stand up for you. No matter what!

Give and it shall be given to you. . . . It will be pressed down, shaken together, and running over.

—Luke 6:38

No matter how little you have, you can give something to help others. When you give, you learn to love others. And you find out how much you can help!

He made the storm as quiet as a whisper. The waves of the ocean calmed down.

—Psalm 107:29

God is big and powerful. But sometimes he comes to you like a whisper. He knows when you feel sad and lonely. And he will comfort you with something small. Maybe a whisper.

A huge cloud of witnesses is all around us.

—Hebrews 12:1

The Christian life is like a race. You prepare yourself by reading the Bible and praying. You keep your eyes on Jesus, and you listen to the cheers of Christians.

LORD, *guard my mouth. Keep watch over the door of my lips.*

—Psalm 141:3

Sometimes we say bad things we don't mean to say. We all need God to help us stop saying bad things. God can help you zip your lips!

Don't have anything to do with arguing. It is dumb and foolish. You know it only leads to fights.

—2 Timothy 2:23

God wants you to stop a fight *before* it starts. One way to do that is not to have anything to do with silly arguments. Just say, "No, I'm not going to argue."

Don't you know that you yourselves are God's temple? God's Spirit lives in you.

—1 Corinthians 3:16

If you believe in God, your heart is his home! He moves in and helps you with everything in your life. He stays close to you and is your best Friend.

Nothing God created is hidden from him. His eyes see everything.

—Hebrews 4:13

God's eyes are full of love. He watches so that he can help you do good. God wants to help you when you are tempted to do wrong.

I will teach you about God's power. I won't hide the things the Mighty One does.

—Job 27:1

The power of the Holy Spirit is free. The power of the Holy Spirit is used to honor Jesus. God sends his power to bring people to Jesus.

When you have turned back,
help your brothers to be strong.

—Luke 22:32

God knows you will mess up sometimes. But God *never* gives up on you. God will always forgive you. And he will use you to help others too.

You bring light into my darkness.

—2 Samuel 22:29

Have you ever been afraid of the dark? Next time you are afraid, think about God. Imagine how bright he is. Then thank him for being your light.

As a mother comforts her child,
I will comfort you.

—Isaiah 66:13

God is like your mom or dad. When you are hurting, he holds you. He lets you cry, and he comforts you. God is better than a Band-Aid!

You are the God who sees me.

—Genesis 16:13

You are never alone. God is on your side. God stays on your side even when everyone else turns away. God has a special place in his heart for you.

God treats everyone the same.

—Romans 2:11

God doesn't love boys more than he loves girls, or girls more than boys. God loves every person just the same.

He calls his own sheep by name and leads them out.

—John 10:3

You feel very special when someone remembers your name. You are special to God and he knows your name. God will never say, "Hey, what's-your-name?"

Won't he go after the one lost sheep until he finds it?

—Luke 15:4

Jesus knows you better than a shepherd knows his sheep. He loves you more. He will always help you. He has promised. He's your shepherd.

The Lord will command his angels to take good care of you. They will lift you up in their hands. Then you won't trip over a stone.

—Psalm 91:11

Next time you are afraid remember the power of love. Remember that God's angels protect you. Remember that God himself has everything under control—even the scary things.

So the cloud of the LORD was above the holy tent during the day.

—Exodus 40:38

How do you know where to go and what to do? God does not send a cloud to guide you. But he gave you his Word. That's better than a cloud any day!

He leads me beside quiet waters. He gives me new strength. He guides me in the right paths for the honor of his name.

—Psalm 23:2,3

God will walk with you. He will calm your soul. He will cover you with promises and fill you with love. You will walk secure in God's goodness.

*Shout to the LORD with joy,
everyone on earth.*

—Psalm 100:1

You can't keep your mouth shut when great things happen. You have to shout! You have to let the whole world know how happy you are!

They are like a tree that is planted near a stream of water.

—Psalm 1:3

A beautiful river flows straight from God. God's people live there. Everyone loves each other. Someday, you will see it. What a wonderful promise!

Turn all your worries over to him.
He cares about you.

—I Peter 5:7

God watches over you! Nothing escapes his attention. He cares *about* you. God is watching over you in love, right now.

Carry each other's heavy loads.
If you do, you will give the law
of Christ its full meaning.

—Galatians 6:2

Some jobs are too big for you to do alone. That's why God gave you a family to help you. You need to help others in your family, too. That's teamwork.

Listen to your father's advice. Don't turn away from your mother's teaching.

—Proverbs 1:8

You will be rewarded when you listen to your parents. Your father knows things that you don't know. Your mother can teach you how to live. Listen to them!

Remember the one who created you. Remember him while you are still young.

—Ecclesiastes 12:1

Spend time with God while you are young. That will give you a head start in life. Then your whole life you can follow God's plans.

All angels are spirits who serve.

—Hebrews 1:14

If you love Jesus, you have your very own guardian angel who watches over you. Thank God for your angel today!

∝

He will strengthen you.

—2 Thessalonians 3:3

When you feel weak, remember this verse. God promises to strengthen you. God is faithful, too. That means God will keep his promises.

I prayed to the God of heaven.

—Nehemiah 2:4

You can pray anytime, anywhere! It doesn't matter where you are, who you are with, what time it is. You can always pray. Because God is always listening!

Think about what is lovely and worthy of respect.

—Philippians 4:8

What you think does not matter. Right? No, that's wrong! God cares about your mind, so fill your mind with lovely thoughts. God will help you.

Obey this rule and obey that rule.

—Isaiah 28:13

God doesn't really like rules that much. He wants you to obey him because you love him. Love God first, and he will help you keep the rules.

You need to get some rest.

—Mark 6:31

Jesus knows that you get tired. And that's okay. Next time you're tired, go to a quiet place and talk to Jesus. He loves to be with you, even when you're tired.

All comfort comes from God.

—2 Corinthians 1:3

God is a comforter. He wraps you in his love. He makes you feel safe and warm. In his arms you can relax and not be afraid.

I will send for you by name.
You belong to me.

—Isaiah 43:1

You are special to God! He bought you. He paid for your sins when Jesus died on the cross. God cares for you because you are very special to him!

*My love for you is so strong
it won't let you go.*

—Song of Songs 8:6

Love is the most powerful thing in the world! Love created you. Love made Jesus come to save you. Love builds up and heals. That's powerful!

It is better to eat a dry crust of bread in peace and quiet than to eat a big dinner in a house that is full of fighting.

—Proverbs 17:1

God says that if you have peace and not very much else, you can be happy. God's in favor of peace.

∝

And she gave him a drink.

—Genesis 24:18

Ask God to help you to be kind.
Then others will know that you
are a loving person, too.

So I always try not to do anything wrong in the eyes of God and people.

—Acts 24:16

Your conscience is what makes you feel bad when you sin. When God forgives you, your conscience won't bother you anymore.

Come. Let us return to the Lord . . .
He will heal us.

—Hosea 6:1

You may not want to talk to God when you've done wrong. But God always loves you. He will forgive you. God's love will make you feel better.

But he has given proof of what he is like.

—Acts 14:17

Love and kindness come from God!
You can see it in the world around you!
His goodness spreads joy throughout
the world.

All things were made through him.

—John 1:3

All things were created through Jesus. He made the sun, moon, and stars. He made earth. He made everything in the earth. He created you! You are his!

You planned to harm me. But God planned it for good.

—Genesis 50:20

Sometimes, even when you are good, someone may do things to hurt you. But God will help you even then. God will turn bad into good for you.

While we were still sinners, Christ died for us.

—Romans 5:8

Think about someone who is really bad. Did Jesus die for that person? Yes. Jesus came to save sinners. He can change hearts and turn badness into goodness.

∝

I will still be glad because of what the LORD has done.

—Habakkuk 3:18

When the going gets tough, rejoice in the Lord! Why? Because God gives you strength. God will not desert you. He will lift you up to hilltops of happiness.

The LORD lives! Give praise to my rock! Give honor to God my Savior!

—Psalm 18:46

God wants you to be happy when you praise him. Don't let anybody stop you from loving God and showing it.

He also made the stars.

—Genesis 1:16

Reading the Bible is like looking at stars. The Bible shines bits of light into the night. Trust the Bible. You will walk in God's light.

He will guard you from the evil one.

—2 Thessalonians 3:3

When you are in danger, remember that God will guard you from the evil one. God promised. And you can count on it!

Love your neighbor as you love yourself.

—Luke 10:27